Are You Hungry Tonight?

Are You Hungry Tonight?

ELVIS' FAVORITE RECIPES

Compiled by
Brenda Arlene Butler

MetroBooks

This book is dedicated to all those
who revere the memory of the King.

MetroBooks

ISBN 0-7607-6302-X

Printed in Singapore by
Tien Wah Press

10 9 8 7 6 5 4 3

PHOTO CREDITS

©American Graphic Systems, Inc.:
    20 (right, top and bottom), 21 (all)
Bluewood Archives: all Elvis photos
California Almond Board: 31
California Milk Advisory Board: 37
California Tomato Board: 6, 22 (right)
California Tree Fruit Agreement: 50
Idaho Potato Commission: 32, 43
National Broiler Council: 35
National Live Stock and Meat Board:
    1, 2 (bottom), 3 (top), 10, 12, 19, 23,
    27, 36 (bottom)
National Pork Producers Council:
    28 (right)
North Carolina Sweet Potato Commis-
    sion, ©Ray Wilkinson, III: 47
Northwest Cherry Growers: 3 (bottom)
Nova Scotia Blueberry Council:
    9, 48-49
©Stock Editions: 14, 25 (right)
Washington Apple Commission:
    41, 44
Washington State Potato Commission: 17

Elvis Consultant: Robin Rosaaen
General Editor: Lynne Piade
Recipe Editor: Meesha Halm
Wedding Cake Consultant:
    Nana C. Brownell
Title Concept: Pamela Berkman
Designer: Tom Debolski

ACKNOWLEDGEMENTS

We'd especially like to thank Robin
Rosaaen, our editors, Lynne Piade and
Meesha Halm, and our typist, Gail Rolka,
without whose help this book would not be
possible.

We're also grateful to both Nancy
Moore of the Aladdin Catering Depart-
ment and Nana C. Brownell, a profes-
sional wedding cake designer, for their
kind assistance in uncovering and inter-
preting the original recipe for the wedding
cake. Thanks also to American Graphic
Systems, Inc.; the California Almond
Board; the California Milk Advisory
Board; the California Poultry Industry
Federation; California Tomato Board; the
California Tree Fruit Agreement; The
Creamery Store, Petaluma, CA; Mabel
Croughan; Dole Packaged Foods Com-
pany; the Idaho Potato Commission; the
Kansas Wheat Commission, Test Kitchen,
Manhattan, Kansas; the National Broiler
Council; the National Live Stock and
Meat Board; the National Pork Producers
Council; the North Carolina Sweet Potato
Commission; the Northwest Cherry
Growers; the Nova Scotia Blueberry Coun-
cil; the Washington Apple Commission;
the Washington State Potato Commission;
the United Fresh Fruit and Vegetable
Association; and Jane Wilson.

Contents

Introduction

The King is dead, but his memory lives on and shines brighter today than ever. No day goes by that his music is not broadcast somewhere in the world. Elvis Presley's impact upon the music and popular culture of the United States—and indeed that of the Western world—was enormous. No other entertainer has ever enjoyed such widespread fame. Each year, on the anniversary of his death, millions of fans make the pilgrimage to Graceland, his home in Memphis, to pay tribute to his memory. And with each passing year the numbers increase. He was the embodiment of the American dream, a young man from humble beginnings who became the King of Rock 'n' Roll.

Whatever his impact upon popular Western culture, Elvis' impact on our cuisine is much more subtle. In this, he was like the king who walks among his people and sits with them to share their repast. Although he became the King, he never forgot his roots. He lived like a king, but he ate like his subjects.

If Elvis were to come into our own dining room tonight, he'd say, "Yes, ma'am," and "Thank you, ma'am," and probably ask for the same kind of good home cooking that his mother, Gladys, put on the table in Tupelo, Mississippi in the late 1930s. Gladys cooked all the traditional Southern favorites. Grits and black-eyed peas were served, ham and bacon were an occasional treat, and there was always fried chicken, cornbread, mashed potatoes, and plenty of homemade country gravy.

Elvis Presley was Southern-born and Southern-bred. His culinary tastes never varied far from Southern-style home cooking, although he was exposed to, and did enjoy, certain Oriental foods that contained such ingredients as pork, with which he was familiar. There was a Chinese restaurant on Highway 51 in Memphis that he visited, and Oriental food was often on the table when he spent time in Hawaii filming two movies and a 1973 concert telecast.

Elvis played hard, worked hard, and ate hard, and he preferred real rib-sticking kinds of foods. Elvis did not develop much of a taste for exotic or foreign foods. Nor did he consider trying any dish that contained unusual ingredients or had an odd texture or flavor. Most of these recipes are, therefore, for honest, hearty food, the kind that Southern women have always fed their tired men at the end of a long day.

Elvis grew to manhood in Memphis during the 1950s in the era of burgers 'n' fries, milk shakes, and soda pop. The Gridiron—an all-night diner in Memphis—was his favorite source of well-done burgers, not only in his youth, but throughout his life. Another of the King's favorite haunts was Chenault's Restaurant in Memphis, which was famous among locals for biscuits and sorghum syrup. Here, in the Delta Room, the King frequently held court with his entourage.

At home, the King always specified exactly what foods should be kept on hand, whether at his Graceland mansion in Memphis or at his house in Beverly Hills. His list always included fresh, lean, ground round, hamburger buns, rolls, at least six cans of ready-to-bake biscuits, pickles, potatoes, onions, shredded coconut, fudge cookies, assorted fresh fruit, canned sauerkraut, mustard, and peanut butter. His refrigerator also contained at least three bottles of milk or half-and-half, thin-sliced, lean bacon, vanilla and chocolate ice cream, and freshly squeezed orange juice. His favorite soft drinks are said to have been Pepsi Cola, Nesbitt's Orange, and Shasta Black Cherry. He liked to chew Wrigley's Spearmint, Doublemint, and Juicy Fruit gum.

If you were to set your table for a meal with Elvis, or even if you just wanted

to create a special meal in honor of his memory, what would you serve? Choose any one of the recipes in this book and you can't go wrong.

The recipes are organized by food type, beginning with breakfast and ending with dessert. Within this, we've included recipes from all periods of his life and experience, from the Southern roots of his early years, to the more complex dishes that were served at Las Vegas hotels.

A sure way to the King's heart was with a big plate of sliced beefsteak tomatoes. Freshly sliced tomatoes were a true favorite of his, and no meal served in his memory should begin without them. The King loved butter and foods cooked in butter. Real butter is, therefore, specified in all the recipes in this book. Margarine may, of course, be substituted, but the recipe will not be authentic.

When the King was in residence at Graceland, his staff made sure the kitchen was stocked with the ingredients for his favorite snacks. Fresh banana pudding and brownies had to be available at all times, and were prepared by the staff of Graceland nearly every night. Recipes for both are included in the book.

But you'll find no fish recipes. Although Elvis recorded several well-known songs about shellfish, including *Song of the Shrimp* (1962), *Do the Clam* (1965), and *Clambake* (1967), he generally avoided fish—even catfish, that great Southern favorite. He even asked Priscilla not to eat fish around him.

Elvis also hated underdone food and ordered his meat "well done." All the recipes herein respect his preference. Microwave ovens were not generally in use during his lifetime, so our recipes all call for the use of a conventional oven.

Elvis wasn't a wine drinker, but he sure enjoyed good food. Some of our recipes call for wine, because wine increases food's flavor. And the alcoholic content of the wine boils away during cooking. You may, however, choose to omit the wine and substitute water or broth.

At some point in the 1950s, Elvis became fond of one dish which is now most frequently associated with him. He probably did not invent the fried peanut butter and banana sandwich, but he certainly made it his signature food. Complete step-by-step instructions for this tasty sandwich are included.

While it was made only once, Elvis and Priscilla's wedding cake marked an important milestone in their lives, and many fans have expressed an interest in recreating it. To this end, we are including complete, easy-to-follow, step-by-step instructions for the legendary cake that was served at the Aladdin Hotel in Las Vegas on May 1, 1967.

This collection of more than fifty of Elvis' favorite recipes will make it possible for you to prepare delicious meals—breakfasts, lunches, dinners, and snacks—fit for the King.

Biscuits and Red-Eye Gravy

SERVES 4

You don't generally find a Yankee starting the day with red-eye gravy, but for folks growing up south of the Mason-Dixon line, there is little question. When Elvis was growing up in that little house in Tupelo, Mississippi, he awoke many mornings to the sizzle and snap of the bacon drippings in Gladys' big black skillet. When Elvis grew up, breakfast ceased to necessarily coincide with morning, but he never outgrew his love for biscuits and gravy.

Biscuits

2	cups flour
4	teaspoons baking powder
2	teaspoons sugar
½	teaspoon cream of tartar
½	teaspoon salt
½	cup shortening
⅔	cup milk

MAKES 10 TO 12 BISCUITS

Preheat the oven to 450°F. In a large bowl, combine the dry ingredients. Cut in the shortening until the mixture resembles coarse crumbs. Make a well in the center and add the milk all at once. Incorporate gently until the dough begins to stick together.

Knead the dough on a lightly floured board for 10 to 12 strokes. Roll or pat to ½-inch thickness. Try not to handle the dough too much.

Cut the dough with a biscuit cutter or slice into squares with a sharp knife. Dip the cutter in flour between cuts. Transfer to an ungreased baking sheet. Bake for 10 to 12 minutes or until golden. Serve warm.

Red-Eye Gravy

	Drippings from 1 pound cooked bacon
⅓	cup strong black coffee

In a large, cast iron skillet, heat the bacon drippings. Add the black coffee. Bring the drippings and coffee to a gentle simmer. Cook, stirring constantly for 3 minutes.

Blueberry Corn Muffins

MAKES 10 TO 12 MUFFINS

These muffins have been a typical treat at Southern roadside cafes since the years when Elvis was growing up.

1¼	cups corn meal
1	cup unsifted flour
¼	cup sugar
1	teaspoon baking soda
½	teaspoon salt
¼	cup packed brown sugar
1	egg
1	cup buttermilk
¾	cup corn oil
1½	cups fresh or frozen blueberries

Preheat the oven to 425°F. Grease a 12-muffin tin with butter.

Combine the dry ingredients in a large mixing bowl. In another bowl, combine the egg, buttermilk, and oil and blend with a wire whisk. Pour the egg mixture into the dry ingredients, stirring until blended. Fold the blueberries into the batter. Be careful not to overmix or the batter will turn blue.

Spoon the batter into the greased muffin tin. Bake for 20 minutes. Serve the muffins warm with butter.

Eggs Benedict for Two

SERVES 2

This elegant dish was a favorite of the King's during his Las Vegas years. It was frequently served to his entourage in his suite at the Las Vegas Hilton, and it was one of the dishes served at the wedding breakfast buffet at the Aladdin Hotel on May 1, 1967. What better musical accompaniment than *Viva Las Vegas*?

1 teaspoon corn oil
8 slices Canadian bacon
1 teaspoon white vinegar
4 eggs
2 tablespoons butter
2 tablespoons flour
1 cup milk
1 cup shredded Cheddar cheese
2 English muffins, split, toasted, and buttered

Lightly grease a large frying pan with the corn oil. Heat over medium-high heat. Add the Canadian bacon and cook until well done, about 5 minutes. Drain the bacon on paper toweling. Keep warm.

Bring 2 cups of water to a boil in the bottom of a 4-egg poaching pan. Place ¼ teaspoon vinegar and one egg in each of the cups, and cover. Cook for 2 to 3 minutes. (If you don't have a poaching pan, cook the eggs for 2 to 3 minutes in a small pot of simmering water to which 2 teaspoons of white vinegar has been added.)

While the eggs are cooking, melt the butter in another saucepan. Stir in the flour. Gradually add the milk, stirring constantly. Add cheese, stirring until melted.

Place two slices of Canadian bacon on each English muffin half. Using a slotted spoon, drain the eggs and place one poached egg on each muffin. Pour the cheese sauce over each egg and serve hot.

Fried Cornmeal Mush

MAKES ABOUT 15 SLICES

Elvis ate cornmeal before he was the King, and indeed before he could walk. Fry up some cornmeal mush and recapture the ambiance of his early years in Tupelo, Mississippi, when Gladys made breakfast for her menfolks on the big cast iron range.

1 teaspoon salt
1¼ cups yellow or white cornmeal
butter
pancake syrup

In a large saucepan, add the salt to 2½ cups of water. Bring to a boil. In a mixing bowl, combine the cornmeal and 1 cup cold water. Stir vigorously to make a thick batter, or mush. Add the cornmeal mush to the boiling, salted water. Reduce heat, cover the saucepan, and cook over low heat for about 5 minutes, stirring occasionally.

Pour the cornmeal into a buttered 8½ × 4½ × 2½-inch loaf pan. Chill until firmly set, about 1 hour. Cut into ½-inch slices. Lightly grease a griddle or skillet and preheat. Fry the cornmeal slices over medium-high heat until really crisp, about 5 minutes. Serve hot with butter and pancake syrup.

Corned Beef, Potato, and Pepper Hash

SERVES 4

Hash was, and is, a staple of Southern cooking. It's a good basic breakfast treat. Elvis liked hash, but he liked his well done, so bear that in mind.

1 teaspoon salt
1 pound russet potatoes, peeled and cut into ½-inch cubes
2 tablespoons butter
1 medium onion, coarsely chopped
1 cup chopped red or green bell pepper
12 ounces cooked corned beef, cut into ½-inch cubes
3 tablespoons chopped parsley
¼ cup half-and-half
3 tablespoons white wine
½ teaspoon dry mustard
black pepper to taste

To a large pot of boiling water, add the salt and potatoes. Cook for 7 minutes, or until the potatoes are tender. Drain the potatoes well and set aside.

Melt 1 tablespoon of the butter in a large, heavy frying pan over medium-high heat. Add the chopped onion and bell pepper. Cook, stirring constantly, for 5 minutes, or until the vegetables are tender.

Pour the contents of the frying pan into a large mixing bowl. Add the corned beef, potatoes, and parsley to the onion mixture. Mix lightly.

In another small bowl, combine the half-and-half and wine. Add the mustard and pepper to taste. Pour over the corned beef mixture and mix gently but well.

Wipe out the frying pan with a paper towel and set it on the stove over medium heat. When it is hot, add the remaining 1 tablespoon of butter. Add the corned beef mixture and press it down firmly. Cook the hash for 15 minutes, or until it is well-browned, turning it once with a flat spatula.

Elvis with costar Debra Paget in a scene
from the 1956 film *Love Me Tender*.

Sweet Breakfast Grits

MAKES 4 CUPS

Grits, specifically hominy grits, is dried corn ground into a coarse white meal, similar to cream of wheat, and prepared by boiling. Grits is Southern soul food. Gladys made grits for Vernon and their little son, and the King's earliest memories of solid food probably included grits. People who weren't raised on this filling staple don't know what they're missing.

Grits is delicious at any meal. Prepare grits for breakfast with raisins and cinnamon.

> 1   teaspoon salt
> 1   cup hominy grits
> ½   cup raisins
> ½   teaspoon cinnamon
>   milk
>   sugar

In a large saucepan, bring 4 cups of water to a boil. Add the salt. Slowly stir in the grits, raisins, and cinnamon. Reduce heat to very low, cover the pan, and cook for 3 minutes, or until all the water has been absorbed.

Serve with milk and sugar.

Glazed Doughnuts

MAKES 16 LARGE DOUGHNUTS

Most folks associate doughnuts with breakfast and morning coffee breaks, but on the road, breakfast and coffee-break time can be anytime, and usually are.

Frost these doughnuts with confectioner's glaze or chocolate glaze. Add toppings to taste. As an alternative, dredge the doughnuts in confectioner's sugar or cinnamon sugar. They're best when served warm.

6	cups vegetable oil
3	cups unsifted flour
¼	cup sugar
1	teaspoon baking powder
½	teaspoon salt
3	eggs
2	cups milk
1	teaspoon vanilla extract

Pour the oil into an electric deep fat fryer. Set the temperature dial at 375°F and let the oil preheat for 25 minutes.

If you don't have an electric deep fat fryer, pour 2½ inches of oil into a deep skillet. Keep an eye on the oil. If the oil begins to smoke, move the skillet from the heat source at once, and reduce the temperature. If the fat is smoking while deep-frying the doughnuts, the outside will burn before the inside is cooked. Return the skillet to the heat.

If you don't have a deep-fat thermometer to test the temperature of the oil, drop a 1-inch bread cube into the hot fat and count slowly to sixty. If the bread browns in just one minute, the fat should be around 375°F, the average deep-frying temperature.

Meanwhile, sift together into a large bowl the flour, sugar, baking powder, and salt; set aside. In another large bowl, beat the eggs until they are thick and lemon colored. Add the milk and vanilla extract, and then add the sifted dry ingredients, beating just until the batter is fairly smooth.

Covering the bottom opening (which should be about ½-inch in diameter) with a finger, pour ¼ cup of the batter into a wide-mouth funnel. When ready to fry, release your finger and run the batter into the hot oil using a slow, wide, circular motion and maintaining as steady a stream as possible. Fry only a few doughnuts at a time and keep them from touching each other. Fry the doughnuts, turning once, until golden brown, 1 to 1½ minutes on each side. Wooden utensils, such as chop sticks, make good turners because they don't retain heat and won't pierce the doughnuts.

Drain the doughnuts on paper toweling. Repeat until all the batter is used.

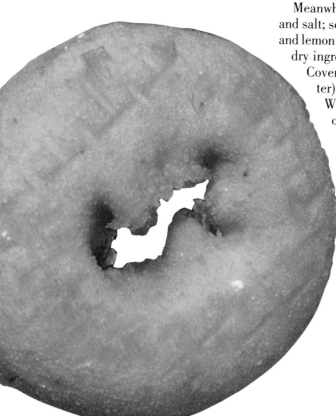

Confectioner's Glaze

MAKES 1 CUP,
ENOUGH TO GLAZE
8 DOUGHNUTS

1   tablespoon butter
¾   cup confectioner's sugar
1½ tablespoons milk
⅛   teaspoon vanilla extract

In a small saucepan, melt the butter. Stir in the remaining ingredients and mix thoroughly. Drop the warm doughnuts, one at a time, into the glaze. Transfer from the saucepan to a serving platter, glaze side up. While the glaze is still warm, sprinkle with chocolate sprinkles, chopped nuts, or grated coconut.

Chocolate Glaze

½   cup semisweet chocolate chips
1   tablespoon butter
2   teaspoons milk
1½ teaspoons light corn syrup

In a small saucepan, melt the chocolate and butter. Stir in the remaining ingredients and mix thoroughly. Drop the warm doughnuts, one at a time, into the glaze. Transfer from the saucepan to a serving platter, glaze side up. While the glaze is still warm, sprinkle with chocolate sprinkles, chopped nuts, or grated coconut.

Elvis assures his fans that all is well upon his discharge from the U.S. Army in March 1960.

Burnt Bacon & Mustard On Toasted Rye

MAKES 1 SANDWICH

Why burnt bacon? Saying "burnt" to the cooks insured that Elvis' bacon would come out the way he liked it, not under done.

6 slices bacon
2 slices rye bread
2 teaspoons prepared mustard

Grill bacon until it is very well done. Drain on paper toweling and keep warm.

Toast rye bread very dry. Spread with mustard. Top with bacon and remaining piece of toast, cut in half, and serve immediately.

Country Kitchen Soup

SERVES 8

This soup, or stew, is the essential main dish at any informal luncheon at which the King's memory is evoked.

2 tablespoons corn oil
1½ pounds boneless pork shoulder, cut into 1-inch cubes
1 cup thinly sliced carrots
½ cup thinly sliced celery
1 cup 1-inch cubed potatoes
1 envelope dry onion soup mix
2 tablespoons sugar
salt and pepper to taste
2 beef bouillon cubes
1 28-ounce can tomatoes, drained
¼ teaspoon dried oregano leaves, crumbled
dash red pepper sauce
1 10-ounce package frozen sliced okra

In a Dutch oven or a large saucepan heat the oil. Brown the pork in the hot oil. Then add the carrots, celery, potatoes, soup mix, sugar, salt, pepper, 4 cups of boiling water, and the bouillon cubes, and mix well. Cover the pan and simmer over medium heat for 10 minutes.

Coarsely chop the tomatoes, and then add them to the soup with the oregano and red pepper sauce. Bring to a boil, reduce the heat, cover the pan, and simmer for 40 to 45 minutes. Gently stir in the okra for the last 15 minutes of cooking time. Serve hot with crackers or cornbread.

Potato Cheese Soup

SERVES 4

Another lunchtime favorite, potato cheese soup has that good hearty "stick-to-your-ribs" flavor that Elvis loved.

2 tablespoons butter
⅓ cup thinly chopped celery
⅓ cup thinly chopped onion
4 cups peeled russet potatoes, cut into ½-inch cubes
3 cups chicken broth
2 cups milk
1½ teaspoons salt
¼ teaspoon pepper
dash paprika
2 cups shredded sharp Cheddar cheese
French fried onion rings or croutons (optional)

In a large saucepan, melt the butter. Add the celery and onion and cook over medium heat, stirring frequently, until tender. Add the potatoes and chicken broth. Simmer until the potatoes are tender, about 10 minutes.

Pour the mixture into a blender and blend until smooth. Return to the saucepan. Stir in the milk and seasonings. Heat through. Add the cheese, stirring until it has melted.

Pour the soup into bowls and garnish with French-fried onion rings or croutons, if desired.

Sausage Spoon Bread

SERVES 6

Cornmeal and sausage are both time-honored ingredients in the down-home Southern cooking that the King loved. Nothing would be cozier on a rainy day than to curl up with a big plate of sausage spoon bread, especially with Elvis singing *Let Me Be Your Teddy Bear* in the background.

1	pound sausage links
4	cups milk
1	cup yellow cornmeal
2	tablespoons butter
½	teaspoon salt
2	tablespoons chopped onion
1	tablespoon prepared mustard
½	cup grated Cheddar cheese
4	eggs, well beaten

Preheat the oven to 425°F. Generously butter a 1¼-quart ovenproof baking dish.

In a frying pan, over high heat, brown the sausage. Drain the sausage on paper toweling.

In the top of a double boiler, heat the milk over boiling water. Gradually stir in the cornmeal and cook, stirring often, until the mixture is the consistency of mush. Add the butter and salt to the cornmeal mixture and mix well.

In a large mixing bowl, combine the onion, mustard, and cheese to the beaten eggs. Gradually stir the cornmeal mixture into the egg mixture. Pour it into the prepared baking dish. Top with the sausage and bake for 45 minutes. Serve with greens and sliced tomatoes.

Quick and Easy Bratwurst Sandwiches

MAKES 4 SANDWICHES

Elvis grew up with sausage, but he probably developed a taste for bratwurst when he was in Germany with the U.S. Army in 1958 and 1959.

4	fully cooked bratwurst
1	teaspoon corn oil
½	cup finely chopped red bell pepper
1	8-ounce can sauerkraut, drained
½	cup Rhine wine or sweet white wine
½	teaspoon caraway seeds
4	French rolls, split

Heat a large nonstick frying pan over medium heat. Add the bratwurst and brown, turning occasionally. Push the bratwurst to one side of the pan. Add the oil and red pepper. Cook, stirring, for 1 minute. Stir in the sauerkraut and continue cooking 1 minute. Add the wine and caraway seeds. Cover the pan tightly, reduce heat, and cook over low heat for 9 minutes.

Toast the French rolls, if desired. Place a bratwurst in each French roll and top each with an equal portion of the sauerkraut mixture.

BLT with Cheese Sandwich

MAKES 1 SANDWICH

Elvis loved a good BLT, probably because two of the ingredients were at the top of his roster of favorites: bacon and big old juicy beefsteak tomatoes. He loved tomatoes. While you're assembling this sandwich, you may want to put *Just For You* on the record player. And remember: Elvis preferred well-done bacon, not actually burned to charcoal, but cooked very crispy.

1½   tablespoons mayonnaise
2   slices white bread, toasted dry
3   lettuce leaves
2   ¼-inch slices of tomato
1   slice Cheddar, American, or Swiss cheese
4   slices bacon, well-done and drained

To assemble the sandwich, spread the mayonnaise on both slices of toast. Top one slice with lettuce, tomato, cheese, and bacon. Top with remaining slice of toast. Cut in half and serve immediately.

To serve hot: In a lightly greased frying pan, grill the tomato slices. Remove from the frying pan. Butter the toast slices on one side and put one slice butter-side down in the frying pan. Top with cheese, grilled tomatoes, bacon, and the second piece of cheese, omitting the lettuce. Top with the other piece of buttered toast and grill to golden brown on both sides. Cut in half and serve immediately.

Fried Peanut Butter and Banana Sandwich

MAKES 1 SANDWICH

Elvis made it famous. He made it part of American folk cuisine. He referred to it as a peanut butter and 'nanner sandwich, and his love for this treat helped to transform this simple delicacy into his signature dish. He loved these sandwiches and would ask that they be prepared for him at all hours of the day and night.

As the basis for a good, hearty lunch, or even as an energy-packed snack, nothing can beat this crunchy grilled sandwich. These step-by-step instructions will insure an authentic peanut butter and 'nanner sandwich.

1 small ripe banana
2 slices white bread
3 tablespoons peanut butter
2 tablespoons butter

1) In a small bowl, mash the banana with the back of a spoon.

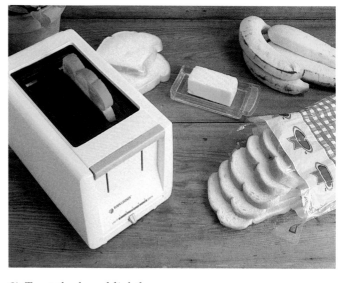

2) Toast the bread lightly.

3) Spread the peanut butter on one piece of toast and the mashed banana on the other.

4) Fry the sandwich in melted butter until each side is golden brown. Cut diagonally and serve hot.

Cubed Beef Steaks with Fresh Tomato Sauce

SERVES 2

A dinner table set for a king deserves a main dish like this one, which is cooked with a man-sized appetite in mind.

3	tablespoons flour
1½	teaspoons dried basil leaves, crumbled
½	teaspoon black pepper
4	teaspoons olive oil
4	4-ounce cubed beef steaks
¾	teaspoons salt
¼	cup finely chopped onion
2	garlic cloves, finely chopped
2	medium tomatoes, seeded and chopped
1	tablespoon red wine vinegar

Combine the flour with ½ teaspoon of basil and the pepper. Dredge the steaks in the mixture. Discard any excess flour. In a large, nonstick skillet, over medium-high heat, brown the steaks in 2 teaspoons of oil. Cook the steaks two at a time for 3 to 4 minutes, turning once. Remove the steaks to a warm serving platter and sprinkle with ½ teaspoon salt; keep warm.

Add the remaining oil to the frying pan. Add the onion and garlic and cook for 2 minutes, stirring constantly. Add the tomatoes, vinegar, remaining basil, and salt and cook, stirring for 4 to 5 minutes. Spoon the sauce over the steaks and serve immediately.

Meat Loaf with Mushroom Gravy

SERVES 6

Meat loaf is basic. Meat loaf is real food, and with mashed potatoes (page 43), how could you go wrong? It was surely one of Elvis' favorite dishes.

Meat Loaf

2	pounds ground beef
1	cup soft bread crumbs
1	egg
¼	teaspoon salt
¼	teaspoon black pepper

Preheat the oven to 350°F. Combine the ground beef, bread crumbs, egg, salt, and pepper. Mix thoroughly. Shape the beef mixture into an 8½ × 4½ × 2½-inch loaf. Bake in an open roasting pan for 1 hour. While the meat loaf is cooking, prepare the gravy.

Mushroom Gravy

2	tablespoons butter
2	cups thinly sliced mushrooms
4	tablespoons finely chopped onion
2	cups beef broth
2	tablespoons cornstarch

MAKES 3 CUPS

In a medium saucepan, melt the butter over low heat. Add the mushrooms and onion and cook over medium heat, stirring until tender. Add the beef broth and simmer for 5 minutes, stirring occasionally. In a small bowl combine the cornstarch with 4 tablespoons cold water. Add to the mushroom mixture. Cook and stir for 1 minute, or until the gravy thickens.

Beef Rib Roast with Oven-Browned Vegetables

SERVES 6 TO 8

It is Sunday noon in America's heartland. Three and perhaps four generations come together after church. The week's big meal is on the table. This was the meal of the week that Elvis looked forward to.

3 cloves garlic, finely chopped
1½ teaspoons black pepper
1 3-to-4-rib beef rib roast
8 small red potatoes, boiled
8 carrots, boiled and cut into 2-inch pieces

Preheat the oven to 325°F. Combine the garlic and black pepper; rub into the roast. Place roast, fat side up, in an open roasting pan. Insert a meat thermometer in the thickest part, but not resting in fat or on bone. Roast to the desired degree of doneness. Allow 23 to 25 minutes per pound for rare, 27 to 30 minutes for medium and 32 to 35 minutes for well done.

Remove the roast when the meat thermometer registers 135°F for rare; 155°F for medium; and 165°F for well done. Allow the roast to stand 15 to 20 minutes in a warm place before carving.

Meanwhile, remove all but 2 tablespoons of drippings from the roasting pan. Add the potatoes and carrots and brown over medium-high heat for 5 minutes. Serve the carved roast with the vegetables.

Homestyle Pot Roast

SERVES 6

Like legions of other housewives of her era, Gladys would put a pot roast on the table when kin were in town. It was a time for a good dish and a good time.

3 pounds beef chuck, tied for pot roasting
1 tablespoon flour
2 tablespoons corn oil
4 onions, coarsely chopped
1 cup beef stock
1 cup canned crushed tomatoes
salt and pepper to taste
¼ teaspoon dried red chili flakes

Dredge the chuck roast in the flour. In a large, heavy pot heat the oil. Put the roast in the pan and sear it on all sides. Remove the meat from the pan and set aside.

Add the onions to the pan and cook, stirring frequently, until they are soft. If they begin to stick before they are cooked, add a little water. Return the meat to the pan. Pour in the beef stock and the crushed tomatoes. Add the salt, pepper, and dried chili flakes. Bring to a boil, cover the pan, reduce the heat to low and simmer the pot roast until it is tender, 2 to 3 hours.

Slice the pot roast. Arrange the slices on a serving platter. Pour some gravy over the meat and serve the rest in a bowl.

Cheeseburgers with the Works

MAKES 4 CHEESEBURGERS

Elvis as Pacer Burton in his 1960 film *Flaming Star*.

Elvis loved burgers, well-done burgers—mainly *cheese*burgers. And the cheese he liked best was American cheese. He and the boys would go out for burgers at all hours. And in Memphis, the expedition would usually wind up at the Gridiron Restaurant on U.S. Highway 51 (now Elvis Presley Boulevard).

1	pound ground beef
¼	cup finely chopped onion
1	teaspoon garlic salt
1	teaspoon oregano
¼	teaspoon black pepper
4	slices American cheese
4	hamburger buns
	lettuce
	prepared mustard
	mayonnaise or salad dressing
	pickles
	sliced tomatoes
	sliced red onions

Prepare the barbecue and let the coals get nice and hot for 20 minutes, or until they look gray-white.

In a mixing bowl, combine the ground beef, onion, garlic salt, oregano, and black pepper. Shape into 4 patties.

Grill or broil for 5 to 7 minutes on a side until the burgers are well done. About 2 minutes before the second side is finished, add one slice of American cheese to each burger.

Serve the burgers on the buns with lettuce, mustard, mayonnaise or salad dressing, pickles, tomatoes, and sliced red onions.

In a pinch, cook the patties in the broiler for approximately the same time.

Elvis enjoys a quick lunch break with costar Debra Paget during the filming of *Love Me Tender*.

Baked Country-Cured Ham

SERVES 8 TO 10

Holidays particularly were special at Graceland. It was at holidays that the King came home from filming movies in Hollywood, or performing in Las Vegas. Ham is for those special times, like Christmas dinner. Why not spend Christmas with Elvis? Invite your friends to bring their special memories of the King. Put a country ham in the oven, and some of his Christmas songs—from *White Christmas* to *Blue Christmas*—on the record player.

1   country-cured ham, 5 to 7 pounds
      whole cloves
½   cup cider vinegar
½   tablespoon Worcestershire sauce
1   bay leaf
½   cup molasses

Preheat the oven to 325°F. Remove the rind from the ham without removing the delicate layer of fat. Gently wash the ham under running water. Pat dry. Score the fat into diamond shapes and place a whole clove in the center of each diamond. Insert a meat thermometer into a meaty part of the ham, being careful that the thermometer stem does not touch bone.

    Place the ham, fat side up, in a large roasting pan with a cover. Heavy-duty foil may be used to make a cover, if necessary. In a bowl, combine 3 cups of hot water, the vinegar, and Worcestershire sauce and pour it over the ham. Float the bay leaf in the sauce on the bottom of the roasting pan. Bake for 20 minutes per pound or to an internal temperature of 160°F. Baste often with molasses. Uncover the ham during the last 30 minutes of baking. Let it stand 10 minutes before slicing.

Ham Slice with Saucy Apple Wedges

SERVES 4

Smoked ham is great for late night snacks (and goodness knows the King was fond of late night snacks). This recipe is a creative way to prepare a slice of smoked ham.

1	pound fully cooked smoked ham slice, cut ¾- to 1-inch thick
1	small cooking apple, cored and cut into thin wedges
1	tablespoon butter
1	cup apple juice
2	tablespoons brown sugar
2	tablespoons raisins
1	tablespoon lemon juice
1½	teaspoons cornstarch
¾	teaspoon ground cinnamon
¼	teaspoon ground ginger
¼	teaspoon dry mustard

Place the ham slice on a rack in the broiler pan so the surface of the ham is 4 to 5 inches from the heat source. Broil for 15 minutes, turning once.

Meanwhile, in a large frying pan, cook over medium heat the apple wedges in butter for 3 minutes.

In a small bowl, combine the apple juice, brown sugar, raisins, lemon juice, cornstarch, cinnamon, ginger, and mustard. Add to the apples and cook, uncovered, for 5 minutes, stirring constantly, until the sauce thickens. Serve with the ham.

Mississippi Barbecued Pork

SERVES 6

Plan a party the way Elvis and his boys would have done it in the good ol' days. Fry up some breaded onions, rewind the tape to *See See Rider* and rock 'n' roll!

2½   pounds butt pork roast
1   teaspoon corn oil
1   4-ounce can tomato sauce
¼   cup cider vinegar
¼   cup Worcestershire sauce
¼   cup brown sugar
    salt and pepper to taste
½   teaspoon celery seeds
½   teaspoon chili powder
    dash red pepper sauce

Randomly pierce the surface of the roast with a sharp knife. In a Dutch oven, over high heat, brown the roast on all sides in the corn oil. In a mixing bowl, combine the remaining ingredients and mix well. Pour the mixture over the roast and bring to a boil. Reduce heat, cover, and simmer, basting frequently for 2 hours, or until pork is fork tender. Let the roast stand for 10 minutes before slicing.

Backyard Barbecue Spareribs

SERVES 4

Summertime was always backyard barbecue time, a time for friends to get together for a plate of ribs and a glass of iced tea. When you have a five-acre back yard, it makes for some mighty big barbecues and plenty of friends. Even the King himself was known to handle a spatula at the big parties in Memphis.

4 pounds pork spareribs
1 cup catsup
salt and pepper to taste
¼ cup Worcestershire sauce
1½ cups cherry cola soft drink
¼ cup vinegar
2 teaspoons paprika
2 teaspoons chili powder
1 medium onion, finely chopped

Cut ribs into serving-size pieces and place on grill over gray-white coals. Cook slowly for 1 to 1¼ hours, turning often with the tongs.

Combine the remaining ingredients in a saucepan and simmer for 10 to 15 minutes. Brush the ribs generously with the sauce and continue to cook, for about 30 minutes, basting and turning often.

Old-Fashioned Scrapple

SERVES 6 TO 8

Many of the great "old-fashioned" dishes survive in the cuisine of the South. Scrapple is one of these, a good solid dish to satisfy a good solid American appetite. Try serving it for lunch with catsup and creamed onions.

1 pound cooked, boned pork loin, chopped
1 cup cornmeal
1 14½-ounce can chicken broth
¼ teaspoon dried thyme
¼ teaspoon salt
½ cup all-purpose flour
¼ teaspoon pepper
2 tablespoons corn oil

In a large saucepan, combine the pork, cornmeal, chicken broth, thyme, and salt. Bring to a boil, over medium heat, stirring often. Reduce heat and simmer, stirring constantly, for 2 minutes or until the mixture is very thick. Remove the pan from the heat.

Line an 8×8×2-inch baking pan with waxed paper, letting the paper extend 3 to 4 inches above the top of the pan. Spoon the pork mixture into the pan. Cover and chill in the refrigerator overnight.

Unmold. Cut the scrapple into squares. Combine the flour and pepper. Dust the squares with the flour mixture.

In a large skillet, heat the oil and brown the scrapple on both sides. Serve hot.

Pork Chops and Sweet Potatoes

SERVES 4

Pork chops are great for breakfast, lunch, or dinner. Elvis liked his well-done, and he'd eat them as any Southerner would, with applesauce, grits, eggs, mashed potatoes, green beans, black-eyed peas, fried okra, sliced tomatoes, sweet corn, creamed onions, or with sweet potatoes, one of his favorite foods.

Put *Guitar Man* on the tape deck and dig in.

⅛ teaspoon salt
⅛ teaspoon black pepper
¾ cup all-purpose flour
2 teaspoons corn oil
4 pork loin chops, cut ¾- to 1-inch thick
4 cooked sweet potatoes, cut into small chunks
1 tablespoon butter
½ cup currant jelly
½ cup orange juice
1 tablespoon lemon juice
   grated rind of one lemon
1 teaspoon dry mustard
1 teaspoon paprika
½ teaspoon ground ginger

Preheat the oven to 350°F. Combine the salt, pepper, and flour in a shallow pie pan. Dredge the chops in the flour mixture.

Heat the oil in a frying pan and brown the chops in the oil, and then transfer them to a shallow baking dish. Arrange the sweet potatoes around the chops.

In a saucepan, combine the remaining ingredients and simmer, stirring, for 3 minutes. Pour ¾ cup of the sauce over the chops and sweet potatoes. Bake uncovered for 40 to 45 minutes, basting frequently with the remaining sauce.

Skillet Almond Pork

SERVES 4

Skillet Almond Pork might seem to be a far cry from pork chops, but the basic ingredient is clearly the same. Elvis' taste seldom departed far from Southern-style home cooking, but he was willing to try a new dish if the main ingredient was familiar.

¾ pound pork tenderloin
1 teaspoon crumbled tarragon
1 teaspoon garlic salt
3 tablespoons butter
2 tablespoons flour
¾ cup white wine
1 chicken bouillon cube, crumbled
1 tablespoon Dijon mustard
¼ cup whipping cream
½ cup toasted, slivered almonds
¼ cup sliced green onions

Slice the pork ½-inch thick. Using a mallet, pound the pork between sheets of waxed paper to approximately ¼-inch thick. Combine the tarragon and garlic salt. Sprinkle over the meat and rub in. Let stand for 1 hour.

Heat 1 tablespoon of the butter in a large skillet. Add the pork, a few slices at a time. Brown them quickly on both sides, about 2 minutes. Put the pork on a serving platter and keep warm.

Add the remaining 2 tablespoons of butter to the skillet. Blend in the flour. Add the wine, bouillon cube, and mustard. Bring to a boil and cook, stirring, for 1 minute. Reduce the heat and stir in the cream. Heat through. Stir in the almonds and green onions, reserving 1 tablespoon of each. Pour the sauce over the pork. Garnish with the reserved almonds and green onions.

Basic Fried Chicken

SERVES 4

Whatever the highlights and nuances of Southern cuisine, there is no dish more universal than fried chicken.

Gladys cooked fried chicken when Elvis was still a little pup. He cut his teeth on fried chicken, and ate it all his life. Put *Big Boss Man* on the turntable, close your eyes, smell the chicken frying, and imagine that the King will be coming in the door any minute.

> 1   fryer chicken, cut into serving parts
> ½   cup flour
> 1   teaspoon salt
> ¼   teaspoon pepper
>   corn oil

Combine the flour, salt, and pepper in a paper bag. Rinse the chicken in cold running water and pat it dry with a paper towel. Drop two or three pieces of chicken at a time into the flour mixture and shake the bag to coat it well.

Heat the oil, about ½-inch deep, in a large, heavy frying pan, over medium-high heat, until a drop of water sizzles when added to the oil. Place the chicken pieces skin side down, into the hot oil, being careful not to crowd them. Cook until golden brown. Turn the pieces over and reduce the heat to medium-low. Cover the pan and cook until the chicken is tender, about 30 minutes.

Drain the fried chicken on paper toweling, and serve with gravy.

Chicken Gravy

        3 to 4 tablespoons flour
        ½   cup milk
        ¼   teaspoon salt
        ¼   teaspoon black pepper

Make a rich gravy from the drippings left in the skillet after frying the chicken. Pour off the excess fat, leaving 3 to 4 tablespoons of fat and the bits of meat. Over medium heat, stir 3 tablespoons of flour into the drippings, and brown the flour, stirring constantly, until it is golden.

In the top of a double boiler, scald the milk, stirring constantly until it begins to boil. Remove from the heat and slowly pour the hot milk into the skillet, stirring constantly. Stir in the salt and pepper. Continue stirring until the gravy is creamy and comes to a boil, about 3 minutes.

To thin the gravy, stir in boiling water. To thicken the gravy, stir in more flour. Serve hot over mashed potatoes, rice, or with biscuits.

Chicken à la King

SERVES 6

This is a dish fit for the King, from the period of his life when he reigned in Las Vegas. Chicken à la King can be served at a dinner party, and when you put it on the table between two blue candles, only one song will do—*King of the Whole Wide World.*

        1   tablespoon butter
        1½   pounds boneless, skinless chicken breasts, cut into 1-inch
               pieces
        ½   teaspoon salt
        ¼   teaspoon pepper
        1½   cups sour cream
        1   teaspoon soy sauce
        1   teaspoon paprika
        2   tablespoons white wine
        1   5-ounce package of frozen mixed peas, pearl onions, and
               mushrooms, cooked according to package directions
        4   tablespoons freshly grated Parmesan cheese
        6   slices white bread, toasted, and each slice cut into 4
               triangles

Melt the butter in a large, nonstick frying pan. Add the chicken in one layer and cook over medium heat about 4 minutes. Turn all the pieces and cook until light brown, about 4 minutes more. Sprinkle with salt and pepper. Stir in the sour cream, soy sauce, and paprika. Reduce the heat to low and cook until the sauce is hot, but not boiling. Stir in the white wine and cook for 1 minute more.

Add the hot, cooked peas, pearl onions, and mushrooms. Transfer the chicken mixture to a greased 1½-quart shallow baking dish. Sprinkle with Parmesan cheese. Put under the broiler until the top is lightly browned, about 4 minutes. Serve garnished with the toast points.

Quick Chicken Supper Skillet

SERVES 4 TO 6

Imagine it's Tupelo, Mississippi, in the 1930s. The sun is sinking in the west. Vernon is on the front porch, little Elvis is playing in the yard, and Gladys is in the kitchen cutting the chicken up to fry. Then slip the King's own *Little Cabin Home on the Hill* onto the record player.

⅓ cup flour
½ teaspoon salt
¼ teaspoon black pepper
¼ teaspoon poultry seasoning (optional)
2½ pounds chicken pieces (breast, legs, thighs)
2 tablespoons butter
1 tablespoon corn oil
1 cup long grain white rice
1 cup chopped onion
1 cup coarsely chopped carrots
1 cup coarsely chopped celery
1 cup coarsely chopped mushrooms
1 teaspoon crumbled dried basil
1 10¾-ounce can condensed chicken broth

On a large plate, combine the flour, salt, pepper, and poultry seasoning. Dredge the chicken in the mixture. Heat the butter and oil in a large, heavy skillet. Brown the chicken on both sides and remove from the skillet. Cook the rice, onion, carrots, celery, and mushrooms until the vegetables are tender, about 2 minutes. Stir in the basil and chicken broth. Arrange the browned chicken on top of the rice mixture in the skillet. Bring to a boil. Cover the skillet, reduce the heat to low, and simmer for 25 to 30 minutes, or until the rice and chicken are tender.

Elvis portrayed the reformed outlaw Jess Wade in the 1969 film *Charro!*

Savory Chicken Pot Pie

SERVES 6

A good basic all-American dish, chicken pot pie was often served in Elvis' day for a good hearty lunch.

	pastry for a 9-inch double-crust pie (recipe on page 49)
3	tablespoons butter
3	tablespoons flour
1½	cups hot chicken broth
½	cup milk
½	teaspoon salt
¼	teaspoon pepper
½	teaspoon lemon juice
3	pounds fryer chicken, boiled, skinned, boned, and cut into pieces

Preheat the oven to 425°F. Line a 2-quart baking dish with the pastry.

In a large saucepan, melt the butter over medium heat. Add the flour and stir until light brown, about 2 minutes. Stir in the chicken broth, continuing to stir until the mixture is thick and smooth. Slowly add the milk, continuing to stir. Add the salt, pepper, and lemon juice and cook, stirring frequently, until the mixture is quite thick.

Stir in the cooked chicken and transfer to the prepared baking dish. Cover with the remaining pastry. Seal around the edges and crimp. Make several slits in the top crust. Bake for 25 minutes. Let stand about 5 minutes before serving.

Spaghetti and Meatballs

SERVES 4

Almost without exception, when you have a bunch of folks to serve on short notice, nothing pleases more people better than this universal favorite. In the case of the King, *that* was a man and an entourage that loved spaghetti.

Spaghetti Sauce

2	teaspoons corn oil
¼	cup finely chopped onion
2	garlic cloves, finely chopped
1	16-ounce can peeled Italian tomatoes, chopped
1	6-ounce can tomato paste
1	teaspoon dried basil, crumbled
½	teaspoon dried oregano, crumbled
¼	teaspoon black pepper
½	teaspoon salt
2	tablespoons grated Parmesan cheese
1	pound cooked spaghetti

Heat the oil in the skillet. Add the onion and garlic and cook over low heat, stirring constantly, until the onion is tender. Add the tomatoes, and the juice from the can, the tomato paste, basil, oregano, pepper, and salt. Bring to a boil, stirring occasionally. Reduce heat to medium-low and add 1 tablespoon of the grated Parmesan cheese. Simmer, uncovered, for 30 minutes, stirring occasionally.

Meatballs

1	pound ground beef
¼	cup seasoned dry bread crumbs
1	egg, slightly beaten
2	tablespoons finely chopped onion
1	tablespoon chopped fresh parsley
1	garlic clove, finely chopped
½	teaspoon salt
⅛	teaspoon pepper
2	teaspoons corn oil

Combine the ground beef, bread crumbs, egg, onion, parsley, garlic, salt, and pepper. Mix lightly but thoroughly. Shape the mixture into twelve meatballs.

In a large skillet heat the oil over medium heat. Brown the meatballs for 6 to 8 minutes, turning occasionally. Transfer the meatballs to a warm serving dish and keep warm, while the spaghetti sauce simmers.

After the spaghetti sauce has simmered for at least 30 minutes, transfer the meatballs to the spaghetti sauce. Cover the meatballs and sauce and cook for 9 to 11 minutes, stirring occasionally.

Serve the meatballs and sauce over the cooked spaghetti and sprinkle with the remaining Parmesan cheese.

Macaroni and Cheese

SERVES 4

Elvis ate macaroni and cheese at home whenever possible. He loved it homemade, thick, gooey, and made with American cheese.

1	8-ounce package elbow macaroni
2	cups crumbled American cheese
1	tablespoon flour
2	tablespoons finely chopped onion
¼	teaspoon dry mustard
	salt and pepper to taste
1	cup milk
1½	tablespoons butter

Preheat the oven to 375°F.

Cook the macaroni in boiling, salted water until tender. Drain and keep hot.

In a mixing bowl, combine 1 cup of cheese with the flour, onion, mustard, salt, and pepper. Add to the hot macaroni and mix well. Transfer to a buttered 2½-quart casserole dish. Pour the milk over the macaroni. Top with the remaining cheese and dot with butter. Bake for 45 minutes, or until the macaroni is firm and the top is golden brown.

Savory Collard Greens

SERVES 4

Elvis was raised on greens and he loved them. He didn't love them the way he loved cheeseburgers or peanut butter and 'nanner sandwiches, but he never had a song in his show about cheeseburgers or peanut butter and 'nanner sandwiches.

2 pounds fresh collards
2 tablespoons butter
½ pound cooked ham, diced
1 teaspoon sugar
1 teaspoon salt
¼ teaspoon black pepper
2 tablespoons chopped onion

Thoroughly wash the collards. Set aside. In a pan large enough to cook the collards, melt the butter. Sauté the ham until it is lightly browned. Add the collards, ½ cup of water, and the remaining ingredients. Cover the pan and cook over medium-low heat until the collards are tender, 15 to 20 minutes. Drain if necessary. Serve hot.

Creamy Onion Casserole

SERVES 4 TO 6

Whatever the main dish, no dinner in memory of the King is complete without a creamy onion casserole or side dish. He loved onions smothered in creamy sauce, and they are a perfect complement to chicken, pork, or beef.

1 pound small white onions
2 tablespoons butter
1 tablespoon flour
1 cup milk
½ teaspoon salt
½ teaspoon nutmeg
pinch of pepper
1 tablespoon bread crumbs

Preheat the oven to 375°F.

Peel and wash the onions. Put them into a saucepan, add water to cover, and boil for 5 minutes. Drain the onions and put them in a greased baking dish.

In a small saucepan, over low heat, melt 1 tablespoon of butter. Blend in the flour. Slowly add the milk, stirring constantly, and cook over medium heat until slightly thickened. Stir in the salt, nutmeg, and a pinch of pepper. Pour the sauce over the onions.

In the small saucepan, over low heat, melt the remaining 1 tablespoon of butter. Combine the butter and the bread crumbs. Sprinkle the bread crumbs over the onions. Bake, uncovered, for 30 minutes.

Basic Southern Black-Eyed Peas

SERVES 6

The essential Southern side dish, there was hardly a time—either in Tupelo or in Memphis—when black-eyed peas weren't on the table.

1 **pound black-eyed peas**
2 **tablespoons corn oil or shortening**
2 **teaspoons salt**
  butter
  salt and pepper to taste

Dried black-eyed peas are typically soaked overnight in a covered pan of fresh water before cooking.

However, there is another way to cook dried peas that doesn't require soaking them overnight first. Add the dried peas to 10 cups of salted water and bring to a boil. Reduce the heat to simmer, and cook for 2 minutes. Remove the pan from the heat and cover. Set aside for 1 to 4 hours. Drain and rinse the peas in fresh water. Then bring 6 cups of water to a boil. Add the peas, shortening or corn oil, and salt. Reduce the heat to low, and simmer partly covered for 45 minutes to 1¼ hours, or until the peas are tender. Drain the peas and serve them with a large spoonful of butter.

With fresh peas, shell them early in the morning and let them stand in water in a cool place until an hour before dinner. Bring a pot of salted water to a boil and add the peas. Cover the pan tightly and cook for 15 to 18 minutes, or until the peas are tender. Drain the peas and serve them with a large spoonful of butter.

An alternate way of serving black-eyed peas is to put the drained peas in a pan with a slice of fat meat. Then, let the peas simmer a few minutes until they take on the flavor of the meat.

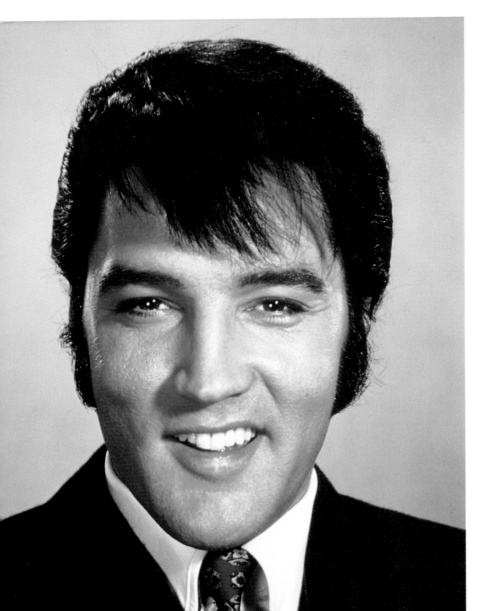

Buttery Baked Sweet Potatoes

SERVES 4

Blue Moon of Kentucky would be a good song to help conjure up the mood of a sultry Southern night and a late dinner: a pork roast and the perfect side dish.

4 medium sweet potatoes
4 tablespoons butter

Preheat the oven to 400°F. Cut off the ends of the sweet potatoes. Bake them until tender, about 45 minutes. Carefully slice each potato in half lengthwise. Scoop the sweet potatoes into a bowl.

Add the butter and mash until fluffy. Then mound the sweet potatoes into the 8 half shells. Serve immediately.

Fresh Kale with Cheese

SERVES 6

Kale is another green much favored in Southern cooking. It's particularly delicious cooked with crispy bacon and American cheese.

2 pounds fresh kale
2 teaspoons salt
3 strips bacon
2 tablespoons flour
½ cup milk
¼ cup chopped onion
⅛ teaspoon ground black pepper
½ teaspoon sugar
1 cup grated American cheese
1 cup soft bread crumbs

Preheat the oven to 375°F. Generously butter a 1½-quart casserole dish.

Thoroughly wash the kale and cut off the tough stems. In a large saucepan, bring ½-inch of water and 1½ teaspoons of salt to a rapid boil. Add the kale, cover the pan, reduce the heat and cook for 15 to 20 minutes, or until the kale is tender. Drain well. Chop the kale into large pieces.

In a large skillet over low heat, cook the bacon until it is about half done. Drain the bacon on paper toweling and remove all but 2 tablespoons of the fat from the skillet. Over low heat, stir the flour into the bacon fat. Gradually blend in the milk. Cook, stirring constantly, until thickened and smooth. Remove the pan from the heat and stir in the onion, remaining salt, black pepper, and sugar. Pour the sauce over the kale and mix well.

Place about half of the kale mixture in the prepared casserole. Sprinkle with ½ cup of the cheese. Cover with the remaining kale. Combine the remaining cheese with the bread crumbs and sprinkle over the kale. Arrange the bacon on top. Bake for 30 minutes, or until the cheese has melted and the bacon is crisp.

Apples and Yams

SERVES 4

Ask anybody south of the Mason-Dixon line to talk about side dishes and yams always come up. This variation on the usual theme brings together two of the King's favorites.

2 large yams
2 well-flavored apples
¼ cup packed brown sugar
1 teaspoon cornstarch
⅛ teaspoon ground cloves
½ cup orange juice
2 tablespoons chopped pecans or walnuts

In a large saucepan filled with water, boil the yams unpeeled for 30 minutes, or until tender but still firm.

When the yams are cool enough to handle, peel them and then slice them crosswise ¼-inch thick. Core and slice the apples the same thickness. In a shallow 1-quart baking dish, overlap the apple and yam slices.

Preheat the oven to 375°F. In a saucepan, combine the sugar, cornstarch, and cloves. Add the orange juice and blend. Cook over low heat, stirring until the sugar has dissolved and the sauce thickens. Pour the sauce over the apples and yams. Sprinkle with the nuts. Bake for 20 minutes, or until the apples and yams are tender.

Fresh Mustard Greens with Potatoes, Southern Style

SERVES 6

Back in the days when Elvis was growing up, people up North didn't eat greens. They ate vegetables. People down South ate greens: mustard, collard, dandelion, and kale. Today, greens are served all over the country, even way up yonder in New York City.

¼ pound salt pork
12 small new potatoes
2 pounds fresh mustard greens
1½ teaspoons salt
½ teaspoon sugar
¼ teaspoon black pepper

Cut the pork into thin slices and simmer, covered, in 1 inch of boiling water for 1 hour, or until tender.

Wash and peel the potatoes. Add to the pork and cook for 5 minutes.

Wash the mustard greens thoroughly, then cut them into 3-inch lengths. Add to the pork and potatoes. Stir in the salt and sugar. Toss lightly. Cover the pan and cook for 15 minutes. Season with black pepper. Toss lightly and serve.

Smoky Mountain Gravy

SERVES 8

Some insiders have told stories about dinners at Graceland where there were mountains of mashed potatoes and bowls of gravy almost large enough to swim in. And those bowls of gravy seldom went back to the kitchen without the bottoms being visible. This gravy should be served hot over mashed potatoes or homemade biscuits.

½ pound mild sausage
3 tablespoons flour
2 cups milk
  salt and pepper to taste

In a large skillet, crumble the sausage and cook over high heat, stirring constantly, until browned. Reduce the heat to medium and sprinkle the flour over the browned sausage, stirring constantly. When the mixture is smooth, gradually add the milk. Continue stirring until the gravy is creamy and comes to a boil, about 3 minutes. Season to taste with salt and pepper. Serve hot.

Heavenly Mashed Potatoes

SERVES 4

Elvis was a meat 'n' potatoes man. He loved mashed potatoes and he loved them best with lots of gravy.

1½   **pounds red potatoes, peeled**
⅓   **cup milk**
4   **tablespoons butter**
    black pepper to taste

Cut the potatoes into quarters or large chunks. Put the potatoes into a saucepan with 1 inch of water. Bring the water to a boil. Reduce the heat and simmer the potatoes, covered, for 20 minutes, or until they are tender. Drain thoroughly.

Add the milk and butter and mash with a potato masher or whip with an electric mixer until light and fluffy. Season to taste and serve with butter or gravy.

Good Ol' Apple Pie

SERVES 8

What is more indigenous to American culture than apple pie and the King of Rock 'n' Roll? Nothing. Not even burgers. Walk through any small town from Washington to Wisconsin and there'll always be pies cooling on windowsills, and you can bet that many of them will be apple pies. And there were always apple pies cooling on the sills in Tupelo and Memphis. Use well-flavored apples like Granny Smith, Rome Beauty, or Pippin.

	pastry for a 9-inch double-crust pie (recipe on page 49)
6 to 8	well-flavored apples
¼	cup sugar
2	tablespoons flour
½	teaspoon ground cinnamon
¼	teaspoon salt
2	tablespoons butter
	cream or milk

Preheat the oven to 425°F. Line a 9-inch pie plate with pastry.

Peel the apples, if desired. Core and thinly slice them to equal 7 cups. In a large bowl, combine the sugar, flour, cinnamon, salt, and apples. Toss gently to mix.

Arrange the apples in the pastry-lined pie plate. Dot with butter. Cover with the top crust. Seal and flute edges. Cut vents and brush top with cream or milk.

Bake for 40 to 45 minutes, or until juice begins to bubble through the slits in the crust. If necessary, cover the edges of the pie with foil part way through the baking time to prevent over-browning.

Sweet Cherry Pie

SERVES 8

When it comes to a good old country pie, cherry is a close second to apple pie. Invite a special friend to join you to share the bakin' as well as the eatin', and put *Sweet Caroline* in the tape deck. Frozen, pitted sweet cherries can be substituted for fresh, but don't thaw the cherries.

pastry for coconut crust (recipe on page 49)
5 cups pitted fresh sweet cherries
2 tablespoons cornstarch
⅛ teaspoon salt
milk or cream
1 teaspoon sugar (optional)

Preheat the oven to 425°F. Line a 9-inch pie plate with pastry. In a large bowl, combine the cherries, cornstarch, and salt. Spoon into the prepared pie plate. Cover with top crust; seal and flute edges. Cut vents; brush top with milk or cream and sprinkle with sugar. Bake for 35 to 45 minutes, or until the juice begins to bubble through the slits in the crust.

Favorite Pecan Pie

SERVES 8

There's no doubt that pecan pie is the pie of the South. Everybody seems to have a pecan tree, and no roadside cafe would mention dessert without saying "pecan pie," unless they happened to be sold out, and in that case, someone surely would have been sent to fetch the fixin's.

pastry for a 9-inch single-crust pie (recipe on page 49)
4 eggs
⅓ cup firmly packed brown sugar
1¼ cups dark corn syrup
1¼ teaspoons vanilla extract
¼ cup butter, melted
1 cup pecan halves
1 cup heavy cream, whipped

Preheat the oven to 375°F.

In a mixing bowl, beat the eggs until foamy. Add the sugar and mix well. Blend in the remaining ingredients and pour into the pastry shell.

Bake for 35 to 45 minutes, or until the center of the pie is puffed and golden brown. Cool. Serve with whipped cream.

Banana Coconut Chiffon Pie

SERVES 8

Imagine you're driving through the South in the 1950s. Your way is marked by the old white U.S. Highway shields, not the red, white, and blue of the Interstate signs. The place names crop up on little white signs, not those huge green things. Memphis. Jackson. Tupelo. Shreveport. It gets awfully hot in the car, so you swing into one of those little roadside cafes for a glass of iced tea. My, but it's cool inside. They've got one of those little glass cases with all the pies displayed, and goodness, doesn't the banana coconut chiffon look good!

As you leave, and push through the screen door, a big Cadillac with a bunch of boys in it pulls up. You chat a bit and they tell you they're headed to Shreveport to sing on the radio—on the Louisiana Hayride. You wish them well and promise to tune in.

	baked 9-inch pie shell (recipe on page 49)
1	envelope unflavored gelatin
3	eggs, separated
1	cup mashed, ripe bananas
⅓	cup sugar
¼	teaspoon salt
½	cup heavy cream
⅓	cup finely grated coconut

Soften gelatin in ¼ cup of cold water. In the top of a double boiler, slightly beat the egg yolks. Stir in the bananas, sugar, and salt. Cook over boiling water, stirring constantly, until slightly thickened. Remove from the heat and add the softened gelatin to the banana mixture. Stir until the gelatin is completely dissolved. Chill the mixture until it begins to thicken.

In a large bowl beat the egg whites until stiff but not dry. In another bowl beat the cream until stiff. Fold first the egg whites, then the whipped cream, and then the coconut into the banana mixture. Pour into the pastry shell. Chill the pie until firm, about 4 hours. Garnish with additional whipped cream and banana slices, as desired.

Lemon Meringue Pie

SERVES 8

	baked 9-inch pie shell (recipe on page 49)
1	cup sugar
¼	cup cornstarch
½	teaspoon salt
3	egg yolks, slightly beaten
2	tablespoons butter
	grated rind of 1 lemon
⅓	cup lemon juice
3	egg whites
¼	teaspoon cream of tartar
¼	cup sugar

Preheat the oven to 400°F.

In a medium saucepan, combine the sugar, cornstarch, and salt. Stir in 1¼ cups of water. When the mixture is smooth, cook over medium heat, stirring constantly, until it comes to a boil. Boil for 1 minute, stirring. Remove the pan from the heat.

Add some of the mixture to the egg yolks, and then pour the egg yolks into the pan and blend well. Cook over medium heat, stirring constantly, until the mixture starts to boil. Remove from the heat and stir in the butter, lemon rind, and lemon juice. Pour the lemon mixture into the prepared pie shell.

In a bowl beat the egg whites and cream of tartar until frothy. Gradually add the sugar, beating constantly, until stiff peaks form.

Spoon the meringue onto the hot lemon filling. Seal it to the edge of the crust. Bake for 8 to 10 minutes, or until the meringue is lightly browned.

Cool for 4 hours, or until set.

Southern Sweet Potato Pie

SERVES 8

This is a luscious sweet potato pie. Be sure to use fresh, not canned, sweet potatoes.

pastry for a 9-inch single-crust pie (recipe on page 49)
⅓ cup butter
¾ cup sugar
2 eggs, beaten
2 cups mashed sweet potatoes
¾ cup light evaporated milk
1 teaspoon vanilla extract
½ teaspoon ground cinnamon
¼ teaspoon salt

Preheat the oven to 375°F.

In a large mixing bowl, cream the butter and sugar together. Stir in the eggs. Add the sweet potatoes and mix well. Stir in the milk, vanilla, cinnamon, and salt, making sure all the ingredients are thoroughly mixed. Spoon into a pie shell and bake for 40 minutes.

Wild Blueberry Pie

SERVES 8

Back up in the hills, the roadside is alive with blueberries and the hill folk put them in everything.

Crust

1½	cups all-purpose flour
2	tablespoons sugar
½	teaspoon salt
¾	cup butter

Preheat the oven to 350°F.

In a large bowl, combine the flour, sugar, and salt. Using a pastry blender or two knives, cut in butter until mixture resembles coarse crumbs. Pat firmly into a pie plate. Bake for 20 to 25 minutes or until a golden color. Let crust cool.

Filling

1	cup granulated sugar
2	tablespoons flour
⅛	teaspoons ground cinnamon
5	cups fresh or frozen wild blueberries
1	tablespoon powdered sugar (optional)
	vanilla ice cream (optional)

Combine the sugar with the flour and cinnamon. In a large saucepan, toss the sugar mixture with 3 cups of berries. Cook over medium heat until mixture thickens. Let cool.

Spoon the filling into the crust. Spread the remaining 2 cups of berries over the top. Serve dusted with powdered sugar or topped with vanilla ice cream.

Pastry for a 9-inch Single-Crust Pie

  1   cup all-purpose flour
  ½   teaspoon salt
  ⅓   cup shortening
  3 to 4 tablespoons cold water

In a bowl, combine the flour and salt. Using a pastry blender or two knives, cut the shortening into the flour until the particles are the size of peas. Gradually add the cold water, mixing lightly with a fork. When the dough is just moist enough to hold together, shape it into a ball. Flatten 1-inch thick.

On a lightly floured board, roll the dough into a circle about 2 inches larger than an inverted 9-inch pie pan. Line the pan with pastry. Turn edge under. If desired, flute.

When a baked pie shell is required, prick the bottom and sides of the pastry with a fork. Bake in a 450°FF preheated oven for 9 to 12 minutes, or until light golden brown. Cool before filling.

Pastry for a 9-inch Double-Crust Pie

  2   cups all-purpose flour
  1   teaspoon salt
  ⅔   cup shortening
  5 to 7 tablespoons cold water

In a bowl, combine the flour and salt. Using a pastry blender or two knives, cut the shortening into the flour until the particles are the size of peas. Gradually add the cold water, mixing lightly with a fork. When the dough is just moist enough to hold together, shape it into two balls. Flatten 1-inch thick.

On a lightly floured board, roll half the dough into a circle about 2 inches larger than an inverted 9-inch pie pan. Line the pan with pastry. Trim the bottom crust even with the edge of the pan. Pour the filling into bottom crust. Roll out the top crust. Cut slits through which steam can escape. Cover the filling with the top crust. Fold the top crust under the bottom crust. Seal and flute the edge.

Coconut Crust

  2   cups all-purpose flour
  1   teaspoon salt
  ⅔   cup shortening
  2   tablespoons sugar
  ½   cup flaked coconut
  5 to 7 tablespoons cold water

Before adding the cold water to standard pastry for a 9-inch double-crust pie, stir the flaked coconut and sugar into the flour mixture. Then continue following the instructions for pastry for a 9-inch double-crust pie.

Spicy Baked Apples

SERVES 4

Nothing's nicer than a baked apple at the end of a big meal. Rome Beauty apples bake best.

<blockquote>

4 apples
¼ cup raisins
¼ cup chopped walnuts
1 tablespoon packed brown sugar
¼ cup lemon juice
¼ cup water
½ teaspoon ground cinnamon
¼ teaspoon ground nutmeg
   whipped cream or ice cream (optional)

</blockquote>

Preheat the oven to 350°F. Peel the apples down one-quarter of the way and core them, leaving the bottoms intact. Arrange the apples in an 8-inch round baking dish. In a small bowl, combine the raisins, walnuts, and sugar. Stuff the mixture in the centers of apples. Combine the lemon juice, water, and spices and pour over and around the apples. Bake, uncovered, basting every 15 minutes, for 1 hour or until the apples are tender. Serve with whipped cream or ice cream.

Spiced Nectarine Cobbler

SERVES 8

Nectarines, freshly picked and juicy, say summertime. Bees buzzing. The smell of the ripe fruit that's still warm from the sun when you bite into it. Close your eyes and imagine Elvis sitting in the porch swing picking out *I Forgot to Remember To Forget* on his old gut-string acoustic guitar. What's that wonderful smell? It's something fresh from the oven.

<blockquote>

8 fresh nectarines, sliced
¾ cup flour
½ cup packed brown sugar
½ cup granulated sugar
½ teaspoon ground cinnamon
½ cup butter
   ice cream or whipped cream (optional)

</blockquote>

Preheat the oven to 350°F. Arrange the nectarines in a buttered 1½-quart baking dish.

In a bowl, combine the flour, sugars, and cinnamon. Using a pastry blender or two knives, cut in the butter until the mixture resembles coarse crumbs. Sprinkle over the nectarines. Bake for 30 minutes or until the topping is golden brown and the fruit is bubbly. Serve warm and top with ice cream or whipped cream if desired.

Pineapple Upside-Down Cake

SERVES 8

There was something about Hawaii that added a new dimension to Elvis' soul. Maybe it was the sun and maybe it was the laid back lifestyle. There's just something about seeing the King in a Hawaiian shirt or a flower lei that makes you know that the place really got to him. Maybe it was the pineapple.

⅔	cup butter
⅔	cup packed brown sugar
1	20-ounce can pineapple slices
10	maraschino cherries
¾	cup granulated sugar
2	eggs, separated
	grated rind and juice of 1 lemon
1	teaspoon vanilla extract
1½	cups all-purpose flour
1¾	teaspoons baking powder
¼	teaspoon salt
½	cup sour cream

Preheat the oven to 350°F. Melt ⅓ cup of butter in a large ovenproof skillet. Remove from the heat and stir in the brown sugar. Drain the pineapple, reserving 2 tablespoons of syrup. Arrange the pineapple slices in the brown sugar mixture. Place a cherry in the center of each pineapple slice.

Beat the remaining ⅓ cup of butter with ½ cup granulated sugar. Beat in the egg yolks, 1 teaspoon lemon rind, 1 tablespoon lemon juice, and the vanilla extract.

In a separate bowl, combine the flour, baking powder, and salt. Blend into the creamed mixture alternately with the sour cream and the reserved pineapple syrup.

Beat the egg whites to soft peaks. Gradually beat in the remaining ¼ cup of granulated sugar to make a stiff meringue. Fold into the batter. Pour over the pineapple in the skillet.

Bake for 35 minutes or until the cake springs back when touched in the center. Let the cake cool in the pan on a rack for 10 minutes and then invert onto a serving plate.

Elvis drums with native musicians in this scene from his 1966 film *Paradise Hawaiian Style.*

Frosted Brownies

MAKES 12 BROWNIES

When the King was home at Graceland, he always specified that brownies be on hand.

Plan a special late-night party around one of Elvis' favorites. Invite some friends, put on *For The Good Times*, and pass the brownies.

1	cup butter, melted
2	cups sugar
2	teaspoons vanilla extract
4	eggs
1	cup flour
⅔	cup unsweetened cocoa
½	teaspoon baking powder
½	teaspoon salt
1½	cup walnuts, coarsely chopped
	Frosting (recipe follows)

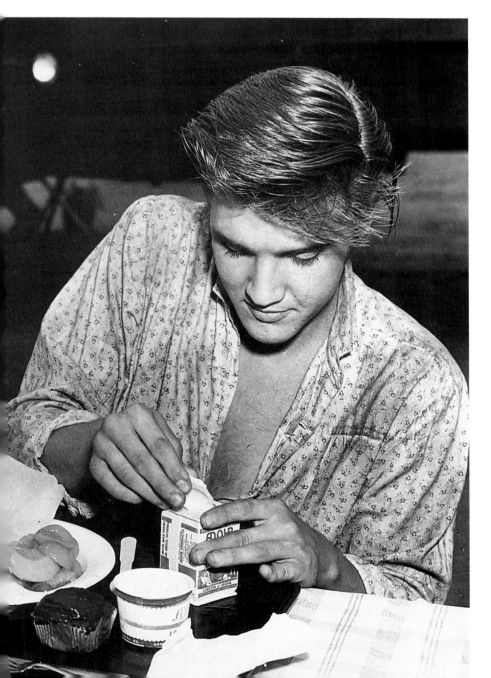

Preheat the oven to 350°F. Grease a 7 × 11-inch baking pan with butter. In a large mixing bowl, combine the butter, sugar, and vanilla extract. Add the eggs and beat well. Add the flour, cocoa, baking powder, and salt and blend well. Stir in the nuts.

Pour the mixture into the prepared pan and bake for 25 to 30 minutes. Do not overbake. Let the brownies cool in the pan. Frost them, then cut into 12 bars.

Frosting

¼	cup cocoa
1¾	cups powdered sugar
3	tablespoons milk
⅛	teaspoon salt
3	tablespoons butter, softened
½	teaspoon vanilla extract

Combine all the ingredients and beat to a spreading consistency. Frost the cooled brownies.

Banana Pudding

SERVES 6

At Graceland, banana pudding was prepared daily so it would always be available for late-night snacking.

- 3 eggs
- ¼ teaspoon salt
- ¼ cup plus 1 tablespoon sugar
- 2 cups milk
- 1½ teaspoons vanilla extract
- ¼ pound box vanilla wafers (approx. 26 wafers)
- 4 medium bananas, sliced into ¼-inch chunks
- 1 cup heavy cream

In the top of a double boiler, beat the eggs lightly. Blend in the salt, ¼ cup of sugar, and milk. Cook over boiling water, stirring until the mixture coats a metal spoon. Remove from the heat and stir in the vanilla extract. Set aside to cool.

In the bottom of a 6½×6×2½-inch serving dish, arrange the vanilla wafers, overlapping them. Top with a layer of sliced bananas. Spoon in a layer of the cooled custard. Repeat layers, with custard as the top layer. Cover and refrigerate 6 to 8 hours, or overnight.

Just before serving, whip the cream, sweeten with the remaining 1 tablespoon of sugar, and spread over the top of the pudding. Garnish with sliced bananas.

Summer Ambrosia

SERVES 8

On those hot, do-nothin' Mississippi summer days, Gladys would sometimes throw a couple of cans of fruit cocktail in a bowl with some marshmallows and grated coconut. Years later, her son was playing Las Vegas and they were serving pretty much the same thing at the buffet there at the hotel. You wonder whether, when the King was on stage doing Little Richard's *Tutti Frutti*, his thoughts ever turned back to one of those good old Mississippi summer days.

- 1 8-ounce can mandarin oranges, drained
- 1 20-ounce can pineapple tidbits, drained
- 2 cups grated coconut
- 2 cups miniature marshmallows
- 10 maraschino cherries
- ¼ cup chopped pecans
- 1 cup sour cream
- 2 bananas, sliced into 1-inch chunks

In a large bowl, combine all the ingredients except the bananas and mix well. Cover and refrigerate overnight. Before serving, add the bananas and toss lightly.

The Royal Wedding Cake

When Elvis Presley wed Priscilla Beaulieu in Las Vegas on May 1, 1967, hearts around the world were broken. The world's most desirable bachelor became a married man, and only a handful of folks were on hand for the event.

For those who weren't present for the ceremony in the second floor suite at the Aladdin Hotel & Casino at 9:40 that morning, or who were unable to attend the reception and banquet which followed, we've reproduced the exact recipe of the wedding cake.

This recipe has not been modified in any way. It is the full-size recipe which will permit you to recreate the entire original six-tiered, pale pink marvel. This cake can be produced for a wedding, for a special occasion, or just in memory of Elvis and Priscilla. For those who wish to recreate a portion of this wedding cake for a more intimate occasion, instructions are also included for making just the top three tiers.

As wedding cakes go, this is a large recipe and the cake should serve five hundred guests. It is not a simple undertaking. Carefully read and study all the instructions before starting to bake the tiers, and make sure all of the necessary equipment is on hand. Plan to spend a minimum of three days making this special cake, especially if you have never before baked or decorated a wedding cake.

EQUIPMENT AND DECORATING SUPPLIES

From a bakery supply store:
cake pans in sizes 8-, 10-, 12-, 14-, 16-, and 20-inch by 2- inches (The 14-, 16-, and 20-inch pans may come in half pans.)
parchment liners to fit cake pans to prevent sticking
1 decorating bag with coupler
stainless steel decorator tips
tip 3 for all string work
tip 4 for lattice work
tip 14 for border around hearts
tip 18 for stars
tip 22 for shell borders
tip 104 rose tip for pink roses, columns, and borders
tip 124 rose tip for red roses
tip 789 for laying a 2-inch band of icing
flower nails
20 9-inch columns
8 Grecian style 5-inch columns
cake separator plates in 8-, 10-, 12-, 14-, and 16-inch sizes
cake circles in 8-, 10-, 12-, 14-, 16-, and 20-inch sizes
    (The 20-inch may not be available, but a homemade cardboard
    round, three layers taped together, and covered with foil, will work
    fine.)
4 sugar bells
48 2-inch sugar hearts
22 1-inch sugar birds
478 silver dragees
210 1⅞-inch silver leaves
20 pounds hydrogenated vegetable shortening (such as Sweetex
    or Crisco)
8 ounces meringue powder

Additional equipment:
  4-speed, 60-quart professional mixer (recommended)
  wax paper
  spatula
  serrated knife
  cardboard tubes from paper toweling or wrapping paper
  cooling racks
  red food coloring
  red piping gel
  old towels to cut into long, 2-inch wide strips

From a party supply rental store:
  36-inch round table, with wheels that lock
  52-inch round white tablecloth to cover a standard 36-inch round table
  pink netting to drape over table
  36-inch plywood round, covered with foil
  round white paper doilies

From a florist:
  fresh Boston fern fronds (to decorate the table which supports the wedding cake)

TO PREPARE THE BATTER FOR THE WHOLE CAKE

Lightly grease all the cake pans and line the bottoms with parchment. Each tier of the cake has two layers, so 12 cake pans should be prepared, more if the larger tiers are baked in half pans.

Combine:

11	pounds hydrogenated vegetable shortening (such as Sweetex or Crisco)
20	pounds cake flour

Always start the 4-speed mixer at the first speed, adding ingredients one at a time until all are incorporated. Then cream together for five minutes at the second speed.

Add:

28	pounds sugar
12	ounces salt
20	ounces baking powder
3	ounces cream of tartar
8	pounds milk

Reduce mixer to first speed and add each ingredient. Increase to second speed and cream together for five minutes.

Add in two parts:

10	pounds milk
16	pounds egg whites
4	pounds whole eggs
2	ounces vanilla extract to taste

Reduce mixer to first speed and add the ingredients in two parts until they are incorporated into the batter. Cream together for five minutes on second speed. Pour about 2 inches of batter into the prepared cake pans.

It is important that each tier is level. Lift the pan a few inches above the counter and drop it. Then, holding the pan in two hands, swirl the batter from the center to the sides of the pan.

Wrap the outside of each pan with dampened 2-inch strips of toweling and pin securely. This will keep the cake level during baking and prevent it from doming.

TO BAKE THE CAKE

Preheat the oven to 360°F. Bake a few layers at a time, taking care not to crowd the oven. Bake for 25 to 40 minutes, depending on the size of the cake pan. Test for doneness with a skewer in the center of each cake.

Cool the layers in the pans on wire racks for 10 minutes. Then run a knife around the edge of each pan and turn the layer out of the pan onto a towel-covered rack. Immediately put a second rack on top of the layer and turn it over so the cake is right side up. There will not be any rack marks to interfere with the frosting of the cake.

After the layers have thoroughly cooled, leave them on the racks, wrap them in wax paper or plastic wrap, and then refrigerate or freeze.

After the layers have been frozen, they can be kept for several days before decorating. If they are not level, use a long serrated knife to trim them before defrosting.

TO MAKE THE ICING

When making the icing be sure that no grease gets into it. Even a speck of grease will break down this icing. It is therefore recommended that metal rather than plastic utensils be used because plastic is difficult to keep grease-free.

Meringue Royal Icing

MAKES 17½ CUPS

This icing is used only for making the decorations. It dries too hard to use for frosting cakes. Always keep the icing covered with a damp cloth because it also dries quickly.

15	level tablespoons meringue powder
17½	ounces warm water
5	pounds powdered sugar, sifted
2½	teaspoons cream of tartar

Combine all the ingredients, mixing slowly, then beat at high speed for 7 to 10 minutes. Put half the icing into another bowl, and using a few drops of red food coloring, tint it a delicate pink. Tint the rest of the icing red to make the red roses. Store, tightly covered, in the refrigerator. This icing will hold for weeks. To use refrigerated icing, bring it to room temperature and then beat.

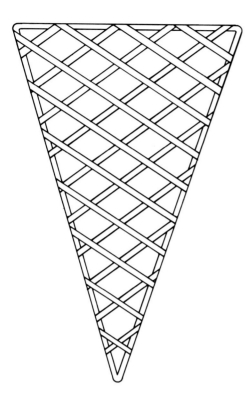

TO MAKE THE DECORATIVE LATTICE WORK AND ROSES

Clusters of red and pink roses, sugar hearts, and lovely lattice work cover the wedding cake. To duplicate the original majestic cake, same-size diagrams are provided to copy and then make your own icing decorations. In all, make:

    58   red roses
    26   pink roses
    26   lattice ovals
    26   lattice half circles
    10   lattice triangles

It is a good idea to make extra icing decorations because they are fragile and might break during the cake assembly or transport. You may also wish to make extra red and pink roses for keepsakes. Gently place flowers in silver foil cups with silver leaves to match the cake. Use a dab of royal icing to attach the roses and leaves to the cups.

TO MAKE THE LATTICE PATTERNS

The lattice decorations are fairly easy to make. Photocopy the patterns on the facing page. Tape this copy to a tabletop or cutting board. Then tape a large piece of wax paper over the copy. This will be the working surface. To make the lattice ovals, use tip 4 to pipe the royal icing along each line, following the lattice diagram. Then pipe the outside border of the lattice.

Next, cut a cardboard tube in half lengthwise. Lay the halves, cut side down, somewhere out of the way where the decoration can dry undisturbed.

Carefully remove the tape holding down the wax paper. Slide the wax paper off the pattern and gently lay the wax paper over the cardboard tube, so that the oval curves in the middle. When the oval dries, it will be ready to attach to the cake.

Attach new wax paper to the work surface and make 25 more ovals.

To make the lattice triangles and half circles, pipe royal icing along the diagrams and allow the decorations to dry flat.

TO MAKE THE ROSES

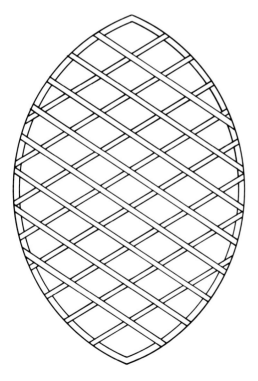

Use the royal icing to make the roses. Attach a square of wax paper to the rose nail with a dab of icing. For the smaller, pink roses, hold the narrow end of rose tip 104, tip up, turn the nail slowly and press out the pink icing to form a full, cone-shaped base that will be the center of the rose. Then, holding the tip at a 45-degree angle, make the first petal by starting at the base of the center, pulling up while gently turning the nail, and then ending with the tip at the base. Add two more petals to make a triangle around the center of the rose. Continue, overlapping five more petals. Surround this bud with seven more petals to form a lovely blossom. This completes the first pink rose. Carefully remove the rose on the wax paper from the nail. After the rose has dried, it can easily be attached to the sides of the cake with a dab of frosting.

To make the red roses, use rose tip 124. Begin as you did for the pink roses. Make the center as before. Then, when making the petals, pull them very tight to the center, overlapping them to make the red roses.

TO MAKE THE FROSTING

Combine:

8	pounds unsalted butter
8	pounds hydrogenated vegetable shortening (such as Sweetex or Crisco)
25	pounds powdered sugar

Cream the ingredients together in the mixer at the first speed until all are incorporated. Increase to second speed for 10 minutes, or until light and fluffy.

Add:

4	pounds egg whites
1½	ounces vanilla extract

Reduce mixer to first speed and add the egg whites and vanilla extract. Cream together, then mix at the second speed for 10 minutes, or until the frosting is light and very fluffy. Use red food coloring to tint the frosting a delicate pink to match the royal icing.

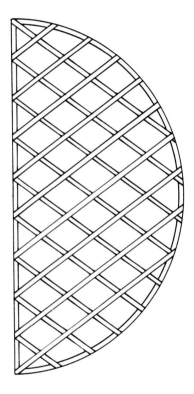

TO FROST THE CAKE

Allow the frozen layers to thaw for no more than one hour before frosting.

Place a cake circle under the bottom layer of each tier before frosting by removing the rack, placing a few dabs of frosting on the bottom layer and attaching the same size cake circle. Mark the center of the cake circles by pressing the same-size cake separator plates into them. The point in the center will leave a pinhole mark that will make it easier to find the center of the tier when assembling the cake later.

Turn the layer over and spread a thin layer of frosting between the top and bottom layers. Then frost the tier, spreading plenty of frosting on the top, smoothing with a long spatula and then generously covering the sides. Blend the edges carefully and smooth the sides. Dip the spatula in a glass of hot water and wipe dry. Run the spatula over the sides and top of the cake until the frosting is smooth. Icing the sides of the cake may be made easier by using tip 789, which will lay a 2-inch wide band of frosting against the cake.

The top of each tier of the wedding cake is textured. This can be accomplished by lightly and carefully drawing a serrated knife blade or cake comb across the frosting.

Allow the frosting to harden thoroughly before decorating.

TO PREPARE THE TIERS

Arrange the tiers in a line from largest to smallest. Mark the position of the columns between each tier by lightly placing the next smaller size cake separator plate on top of each tier except the 8-inch tier. The cake separator plates will leave four indentations in the frosting of each tier indicating the proper position of the columns.

Note in the artwork on the facing page that the cake does not align in the traditional manner. On most wedding cakes, the columns are placed directly above the ones below. On this cake, however, the columns appear to spiral upward.

To achieve this spiral effect, rotate the 14-inch cake separator plate one-eighth of a turn before marking the top of the 16-inch tier. Rotate the 12-inch cake separator plate one-eighth of a turn and mark the 14-inch tier. Mark the

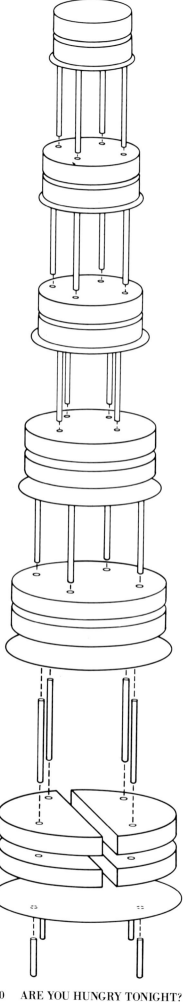

THE DECORATIONS

20-inch tier

Top:
- 4 nine-inch columns
- 4 sugar hearts
- 4 dragees
- 12 red roses
- 24 silver leaves
- 32 dragees
- 20 lattice half circles

Sides:
- 16 lattice ovals
- 16 dragees
- 16 pink roses
- 48 silver leaves

16-inch tier

Top:
- 4 nine-inch columns
- 4 sugar hearts
- 4 dragees
- 12 red roses
- 24 silver leaves
- 60 dragees

Sides:
- 16 sugar birds
- 16 sugar hearts
- 16 silver leaves
- 96 dragees

14-inch tier

Top:
- 4 nine-inch columns
- 4 sugar hearts
- 4 dragees
- 12 red roses
- 24 silver leaves
- 60 dragees

Sides:
- 10 sugar hearts
- 10 lattice triangles
- 50 dragees

12-inch tier

Top:
- 4 nine-inch columns
- 4 sugar hearts
- 4 dragees
- 8 red roses
- 16 silver leaves
- 74 dragees

Sides:
- 10 lattice ovals
- 20 dragees
- 10 pink roses
- 30 silver leaves

10-inch tier

Top:
- 4 nine-inch columns
- 4 sugar bells
- 8 red roses
- 16 silver leaves
- 40 dragees

Sides:
- 6 sugar birds
- 14 letters, piped in red piping gel
  P R I S C I L L A
  —E L V I S

8-inch tier

Top:
- 6 red roses
- 12 silver leaves
- 6 lattice half circles

Sides:
- 14 dragees
- 6 sugar hearts

12-inch tier with the 10-inch cake separator plate, again rotating one-eighth of a turn. Mark the 10-inch tier with the 8-inch cake separator plate and align with the column position of the 12-inch tier.

When the tiers are marked properly, remove the cake separator plates from the tops of the tiers. Gently press the 9-inch columns through the tiers to the cake circles.

TO ASSEMBLE THE CAKE

Using a yardstick, divide the foil-covered, 36-inch plywood round into eight equal sections. Find the position of the 5-inch Grecian columns by measuring 8 to 9 inches out from the center and marking with a pencil where the lines intersect. Attach each of the 5-inch columns to the base circle with dabs of royal icing. Allow the icing to dry for a few minutes. Dab more royal icing on top of the columns. The 9-inch columns should already be in place on the 20-inch tier. Set the 20-inch tier onto the columns, centering and aligning carefully.

The remaining tiers have cake separator plates that snap into the tops of the columns on the tier below. The cake separator plates and columns will give the structural support this heavy cake needs.

TO DECORATE THE ROYAL WEDDING CAKE TIER BY TIER

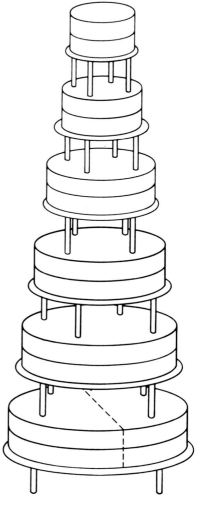

At this point, there are two possible ways to proceed. Either decorate and assemble the cake on the foil-covered round on top of the work surface and then, with the help of another person, carefully move the cake to the banquet table, or, to minimize moving the cake, lay the white tablecloth on the banquet table. Arrange the pink netting over it, and then place the foil-covered round on top. The wedding cake may then be assembled and decorated directly on the table.

Before beginning to decorate the cake, the 20-inch tier should be securely attached to the 5-inch columns. Four 9-inch columns should be sticking out of the 20-inch tier, as well as out of the 16-inch, 14-inch, 12-inch, and 10-inch tiers.

Decorate the cake one tier at a time, keeping the tier you are decorating at eye level. Use rose tip 104 to pipe frosting over the columns first. Add texture to the top of the tier using a cake comb or a serrated knife. Then decorate from the bottom to the top of the tier. Arrange the decorations around the tier before attaching them to the cake. (See the chart at left.) After a tier is completely decorated, place the cake separator plate for the next tier on the columns and gently snap it into position. Then center the tier on the cake separator plate by sliding the tier around until the cake circle catches on the indentation left by the point in the center of the cake separator plate. Follow the decorating instructions for each tier as indicated below and refer to the picture on page 54.

Lay out all the decorations for the 20-inch tier. Use rose tip 104 to pipe frosting over the columns and mark each decoration's position on the tier with a little dot. Space them carefully around the cake, using the four columns as a guide.

At the base of the 20-inch tier, pipe a tip 22 shell border. Then, using dabs of frosting, attach the pink roses, lattice ovals, and silver leaves. Position a dragee at the bottom and top of each lattice oval and gently press into place.

Next, dab some frosting on the back of the sugar hearts and attach them to the columns, placing a dragee at the top of each heart. Pipe another tip 22 shell border 1½ inches inside the top edge of the cake.

Attach the 5 lattice half circles in front of each sugar heart, overlapping the piping. Press 8 dragees into the piping between lattices. Then center the red roses in threes, just inside of the piping, attaching 4 silver leaves in front and 2 behind each set of roses.

On the 16-inch tier, pipe frosting over the columns with rose tip 104. There is no piped border on this tier. Press the sugar hearts into position. Then, using frosting, pipe a tip 14 border around each heart. Place a dragee at the top and bottom of each heart, pressing gently into the frosting. Then using tip 18, pipe 3 stars in a row between the bottoms of each heart.

Use tip 3 for the string work. Pipe a string to extend beyond the base of the tier, bring up and attach to the star and drop again to below the tier, to match the other side. Repeat at each star all the way around the cake. Then press a dragee onto each star. Attach a silver leaf between each heart. Center each sugar bird and attach to the cake. Place sugar hearts against the columns. To complete the top of the tier, pipe a tip 22 shell border 1 inch inside the top. Press dragees into the border and attach red roses and silver leaves as before.

On the 14-inch tier, begin by frosting the columns with rose tip 104. Next use rose tip 104, with its wide base side down, to pipe the bottom border. Place 5 sugar hearts and 5 lattice triangles into place on the sides. Pipe around the hearts as before. Press dragees into place and complete the top as directed for the 16-inch tier.

The bottom border for the 12-inch tier is the same as that of the 14-inch tier. Attach the lattice ovals, pink roses, and silver leaves, again spacing carefully around the sides. Decorate the top of the tier as before, except put 2 red roses instead of 3 in each cluster.

The 10-inch tier again repeats the bottom border of the 14- and 12-inch tiers. Arrange 3 sugar birds on opposite sides of the cake. Then, on the sides of the cake, carefully pipe in piping gel in 2-inch red letters (see photo for lettering style and position) the names of the wedding couple.

Arrange the top of the tier as the top of the 12-inch tier, using 2 red roses in each cluster. Instead of the sugar hearts, attach a sugar bell at the top of each column.

Crowning the confectionery dream is the 8-inch tier. The bottom border is piped with tip 22. Six sugar hearts are arranged around the sides of the cake and a tip 14 border is piped around each one. Press one dragee at the top of each heart. Carefully attach the last 6 lattice half circles to the top of the cake, placing a dragee between each one. Inside of the lattice circle, arrange 6 red roses and 12 silver leaves. The wedding cake is now complete.

TO DISPLAY THE ROYAL WEDDING CAKE

All that is left to do is decorate the banquet table. If the cake was not assembled on the banquet table, cover the table with the white tablecloth. Top with the pink netting. With several strong people, carefully slide the plywood base onto the table.

Arrange white paper doilies over the foil-covered base circle and lay Boston fern fronds around the edge of the table.

TO MAKE A ONE-, TWO-, AND THREE-TIER CAKE

Follow the instructions for the wedding cake but reduce the amount of the ingredients as indicated below. The original cake was made in 2-inch deep professional cake pans, so if only standard 8 × 1½-inch pans are available, use three pans or plan to make cupcakes with the extra batter.

Recipe for the Top Tier only (8-INCH)

1) Mix:

1⅓ cups hydrogenated vegetable shortening

4¾ cups cake flour

2) Add:

3¾ cups sugar

2 teaspoons salt

3½ teaspoons baking powder

½ teaspoon cream of tartar

1 cup milk

3) Add in two parts:

1¼ cups milk

2 cups egg whites (16 to 20 egg whites)

½ cup whole eggs (about 3 eggs)

1½ teaspoons vanilla extract

4) Frosting:

1 cup sweet butter

1 cup hydrogenated vegetable shortening

6 to 7 cups powdered sugar

½ cup egg whites (5 to 6 egg whites)

1½ teaspoons vanilla extract

Recipe for a Two-Tier Cake (8- AND 10-INCH)

1) Mix:

2⅓ cups hydrogenated vegetable shortening

12 cups cake flour

2) Add:

9¼ cups sugar

5¼ teaspoons salt

3 tablespoons baking powder

1¼ teaspoons cream of tartar

2½ cups milk

3) Add in two parts:

3 cups milk

4¾ cups egg whites (38 to 47 egg whites)

1¼ cups whole eggs (7 to 8 eggs)

3½ teaspoons vanilla extract

4) Frosting:

2½ cups sweet butter

2½ cups hydrogenated vegetable shortening

15 to 17 cups powdered sugar

1¼ cups egg whites (10 to 13 egg whites)

3½ teaspoons vanilla extract

Recipe for a Three-Tier Cake (8-, 10-, AND 12-INCH)

1) Mix:

5¾ cups hydrogenated vegetable shortening

21½ cups cake flour

2) Add:

16¾ cups sugar

9½ teaspoons salt

16¼ teaspoons baking powder

2¼ teaspoons cream of tartar

4½ cups milk

3) Add in two parts:

5½ cups milk

8½ cups egg whites (68 to 85 egg whites)

2¼ cups whole eggs (13 to 14 eggs)

2 tablespoons vanilla extract

4) Frosting:

4½ cups sweet butter

4½ cups hydrogenated vegetable shortening

27 to 30 cups powdered sugar

2¼ cups egg whites (18 to 22 egg whites)

2 tablespoons vanilla extract

Recipe for Meringue Royal Icing

The ingredients for royal icing have been halved and will suffice for a one-, two- or three-tier cake. Follow the recipe as before, but use these proportions:

7½ level tablespoons meringue powder

8¾ ounces warm water

2½ pounds powdered sugar, sifted

1¼ teaspoons cream of tartar